Snail's pace to snappy:
How to make your PC fast again

Web of Life Solutions

ISBN-13: 978-1479385386
ISBN-10: 1479385387

This book is also available in Kindle ebook format from Amazon.com and in other ebook formats from Smashwords, iTunes, Barnes and Noble, Kobo, Sony, and most ebook retailers.

Contents

Dedication

For computer lovers everywhere!

Introduction

Our experience comes from over 30 years as computer users, including working as professional computer technicians.

In this guide we'll show you simple ways to speed up a computer that has been slowing down under accumulated bloat and unnecessary processes. And, we'll show you how to keep your computer running at its best.

Don't waste money and time having your slow computer fixed at a computer shop, again and again – learn how they do it in this simple guide – and save!

This step-by-step guide, generously illustrated with actual Windows screen shots, guides you through the simple, quick, and effective methods that computer repair shops use to speed up your Windows computer that has become slow and sluggish. Don't buy a new machine! You won't have to.

Most people don't know these ways to speed up their Windows-based computers, and spend money at the computer repair shop, plus the inconvenience of taking your computer to the shop and waiting to get it back – *all to have the problems that slowed down your computer in the first place reappear. in a short time!* It's a good money-making method for the computer repair shop, but it can get expensive for you!

Or, they think their computer is "too old" and then go out and spend a lot of money on a new computer, thinking they have solved the problem – but it won't be long before they learn they have not solved it. The new computer will start to slow down, too, if regular care is not taken.

What this guide will NOT do is speed up your computer's processor (its "brain"). This guide is intended to work with what your computer has now in the way of hardware, but give you some ways to make the best use of what you have, and improve performance on a machine that was running fine in the past, but has getting slower and slower.

Why Is My Computer Slowing Down?

There could be several reasons why your PC is steadily slowing down, and most of them are reversible, and preventable. We've been running our Windows computers here for years without any noticeable slowdown in performance, or a virus - and we are online daily!

It's just the way Windows-based computer run, that they store a lot of files when you run certain applications. Most of the storage of these files is a good thing – in the short term. Firefox, for example, stores cookies and other files offline (on your hard drive), in order to make your browsing happen in a fast, efficient way. The problems come in when these programs don't delete the files they have stored.

When you delete a file in Windows most often the file is not actually deleted, only the pathway, or pointer to the file is deleted. The file might be deleted at a later date, or when the hard drive is formatted, or defragmented (something you should look into on a regular basis).

Also, Windows stores a lot of log files, that monitor system usage, and can be helpful for debugging, but often grow to very large sizes.

Computers Need Tune-Ups, Too!

If you never gave your car maintenance on a regular basis, it would not be long before your car's performance declined, your gas mileage deteriorated, or your engine even seized up and destroyed itself.

No, your computer will NOT destroy itself if you don't follow the techniques we will give you, but it will certainty suffer a serious performance hit, and have you thinking of buying a new computer – only to have the same problems reappear, as the new machine starts to slow down, too!

What Is Our Secret?

We learned how to use some simple, free software tools and practices to keep our machines running at peak performance. Now, we are going to share these techniques with you, so you too can keep your computers running well for years to come, and stop giving away money to computer stores to fix problems that will only come back if you don't know how to deal with them on an ongoing basis.

Before You Start

Back up your data before you follow any suggestions in this guide! Better to be on the safe side. It's best to keep a copy of your backup files off-site; that is at a location other than your home or office. Make at least two backups of important data, but three is better.

Notice And Disclaimer: Though we will do out best to guide you through making changes to your computer, we will not be held responsible for any damages, or losses, financial, or otherwise that you cause to your computer as a result of reading this guide. The information given here is for informational purposes, only. Please use caution, and when in doubt, don't do it! Never delete any programs from your computer, or change any setting you are not sure of – doing so can impact your computer negatively, to the point that the only solution could be a complete system reinstall. Always back up your data!

NOTE: The screenshots and steps in this guide are from Windows XP Pro, but will be similar for any version of Windows.

Browser Toolbars and Plug-Ins

Most any plug-ins and additions in your browser will slow your machine down. Often, when you install a new program, it will try and install a browser plug-in. We recommend that you do not allow programs to install any plug-ins. Use the manual, or expert installation option, if available. There is one plug-in we do recommend (see later in this guide), but they should be kept to a minimum – and certainly no extra toolbars, or search bars from third-parties.

If you do have plug-ins in your browser, like extra toolbars, or search boxes, then uninstall them from the menu option the program gives, or you may have to disable them from your browser's menu.

To Uninstall Toolbars From The Control Panel:

1. Go to the Start Menu
2. Select Control Panel
3. Select Add/Remove Programs

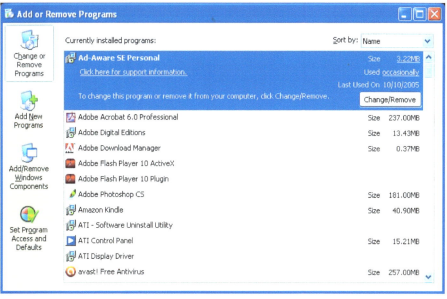

4. Find the name of the toolbar(s) in the list
5. Click Change/Remove.

NOTE: The best practice is to not install them in the first place!

Spyware, Adware, And Viruses

Spyware, adware, and viruses can get into your computer from malicious Websites, email attachments, or sharing files. They can all slow down your computer, so install a good antivirus, adware, and spyware scanner and check your computer regularly. We recommend scanning with more than one, as one may pick up a system infection, or spyware that another scanner misses.

Some good, free ones we've used in the past include:

- AVG http://www.avg.com
- Adaware http://www.lavasoft.com
- Avast http://www.avast.com
- Spybot - Search & Destroy http://www.safer-networking.org

Clean Your Machine

There is a little-known, but almost-magical program called C Cleaner. This is by far the most effective piece of software for keeping your Windows PC in top shape! Developed by Piriform, this **free** software is truly a gift to the Windows-world!

What is does is remove files that bloat up your hard drive and slow down your machine – a lot! We've seen dramatic gains in speed just by running this program, and having a system cleaned by it – alone!

It removes old cookies, log files, downloaded images and text from Internet sessions – and more! Try it, and you'll be amazed at the junk it removes, and how much faster your computer runs!

We recommend running C Cleaner on your machine daily!

Download C Cleaner from http://www.piriform.com

The Piriform Website main page (section).

To Run C Cleaner:

1. Open the program and see the main screen:

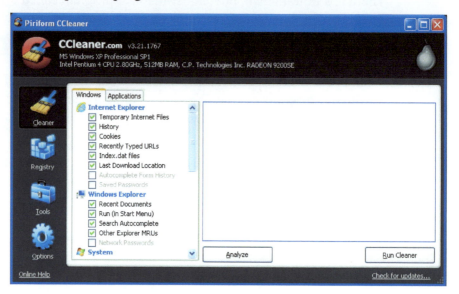

2. In the Windows tab, select the options you want to clean

3. In the Applications tab, select the level of cleaning you want the program to do - we recommend the highest level

4. Click Analyze to see if your system needs to be cleaned

5. A screen displays with the results

6. Click Run Cleaner to clean your PC

7. After that is done, click Registry on the left side to do a cleaning of your computer's registry - this can have dramatic results, too!

NOTE: If this is your first time running C Cleaner, it may take a few minutes to clean your computer. The next time you run the program it should be much faster. You do not have to set the options to clean each time, as the program will remember them.

Cleaning Your Disk(s)

Built into Windows is a handy feature called Disk Cleanup. It can get rid of old parts of install files and also compress files you are not using. We recommended you run it.

To Run Disk Cleanup:

1. Click on My Computer
2. Right-click the drive you want to clean and select Properties
3. The Properties Window opens:

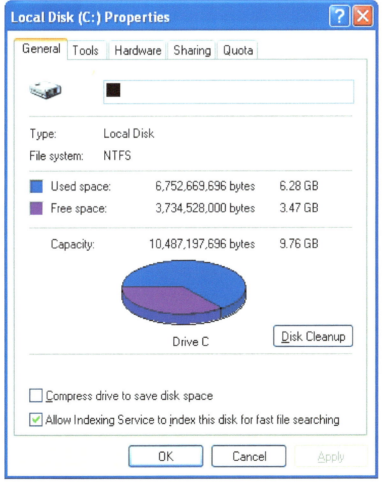

4. Click the Disk Cleanup button
5. The Disk Cleanup Window displays and shows the cleaning progress:

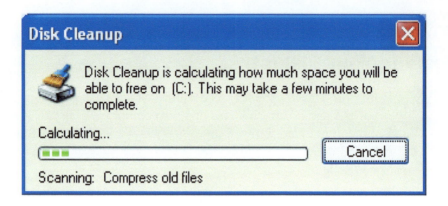

NOTE: Disk Cleanup may take a few minutes to complete, especially if it's the first time you are running it.

What Programs Is My Computer Running Now?

Many programs will start when Windows starts, and this will slow down both the boot time of your machine and its overall performance. Why have your computer start and run programs you are not using? Only have programs running when you need them, for optimal performance.

Press the CTRL ALT and DELETE keys at the same time to bring up the Task Manager. This is a window that monitors the application, processes, programs and other details of your system, such as memory usage and CPU load.

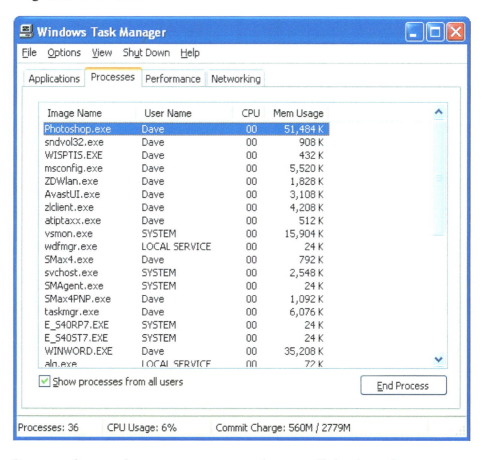

Once you know what programs you need to run all the time, then you can change what programs Window runs at startup - see the next section.

Tweak The Startup Menu

The way your computer starts up can have a big effect on your system's performance. One start up, your computer loads many programs that are essential to your system running correctly. But, it also can start up a lot of other programs that at not needed at that time, and can slow down your computer significantly.

To See What Programs Your Computer Is Initializing At Boot Time, Do The Following:

1. Click the Start Menu
2. Click Run
3. A command window displays
4. Type in "msconfig" without the quotations

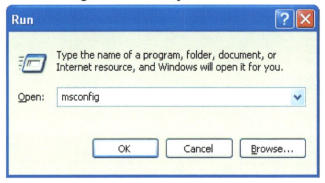

5. A window pops up with several tabs:

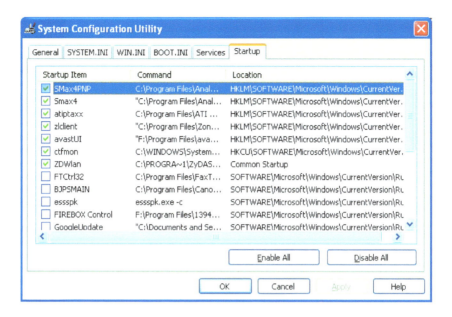

6. Click on the Startup tab

You should now see a list of all the programs that Windows has to start every time the operating system loads. If you see any programs that you don't need to use right away, you can deselect them from running at Startup.

Things like GoogleUpdate have been deselected in the above example, as we don't need this stating up every time the computer boots.

Go through the list on your own computer (with the help of the Task Manager) and look for items that you only use rarely, and deselect them.

When you are done, click Apply and OK.

The next time your system starts, it will not automatically load the programs you deselected. To change anything back, just come to this screen again.

CAUTION! Only deselect those programs that you are sure of! All Windows programs should not be touched, as a rule, unless you are familiar with them.

Use The Right Browser

Using the right browser on your computer can have a big effect. We recommend FireFox, as it tends to let run leaner than Internet Explorer, and has many nice options for keeping your system clean – like the Better Privacy add-on.

Also, Firefox is open source software, which means that it is developed by a team of developers from all over the world, the code is public, and it's free!

Firefox is developed by the Mozilla Project, and takes input from users and programmers all over the globe. Problems with the browser are fixed quickly, and new versions of the program are available regularly.

Get the latest Firefox browser from: http://www.mozilla.org

Once you install Firefox, turn on Automatic Updates.

To Ensure Automatic Updates Are Selected From Within Firefox:

1. Go to Tools
2. Select Options
3. Click Advanced
4. Click the Update tab
5. Select Automatic Updates.

Better Privacy in Firefox

After you've installed Firefox, get the Better Privacy add-on. This will delete Flash cookies that clog up your system, resulting in a slower speed. It's one of the few add-ons we recommend, as having too many can slow down your browsing.

To Get The Better Privacy Add-On:

1. Go to Tools
2. Click Add-ons
3. Search for Better Privacy
4. Download and install
5. Restart Firefox
6. Check the Options tab in Better Privacy and ensure that the option to "Delete all Flash cookies on Firefox exit" is selected.

Mind Your Email

Using an email service like Yahoo or Gmail has a some advantages that will assist in keeping your computer running faster.

First, no email is stored on your machine, so your hard drives will have more space and run more quickly.

Second, your computer will be less likely to pick up any viruses, or spyware via Web-based email, all of which can slow down your computer.

Most Web-based email services these days are free, offer unlimited storage, and have built-in virsus scanners.

Top Web-Based Email Providers:

- Yahoo
- Gmail
- Hotmail

Desktop Icons And Images

The less icons and images you have on your Desktop, the better, as your computer has to load all of these at start up. Consider going without a Desktop background picture, and remove any unused shortcuts.

To Delete Desktop Background Images:

1. Right click on the Desktop
2. Select properties
3. The Display Properties window pops up:

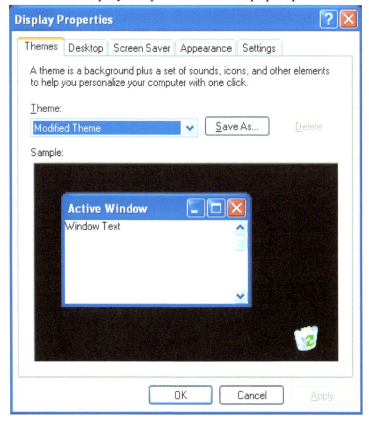

4. Click the Desktop tab
5. Remove the Desktop image - change to none.

Files On The Desktop

One thing that will negatively effect performance is storing large files on your Desktop, so don't do it.

Your computer needs to load up the Desktop every time your computer starts, and if you have large files stores here, it will slow your computer down.

The Desktop is not a file storage location, so use a folder on your hard drive for storage, not the Desktop.

Defragmenting Your Hard Drive(s)

Check to see if your hard drives are in need of defragmentation, and do so if they require it. Hard drives become fragmented, or have pieces of files scattered in different locations, due to both the way in Windows functions, and by adding and deleting files. They need to be defragmented on a regular basis.

To see if your hard drive(s) need to be defragmented:

1. Click on My Computer
2. Right-click on the drive and select Properties
3. A window pops up with details about the drive:

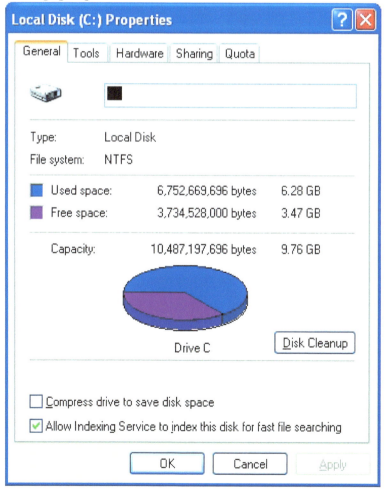

4. Select the Tools tab:

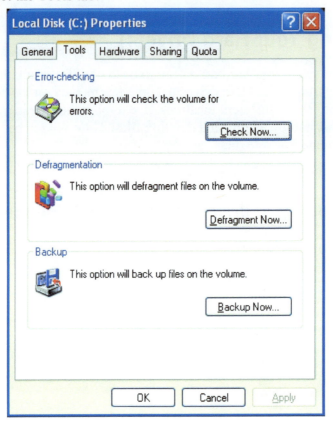

5. Click Defragment Now
6. The Disk Defragmenter window displays:

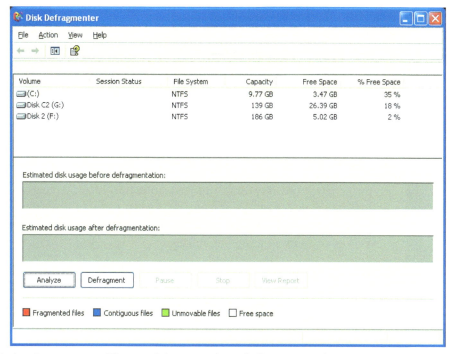

7. Click Analyze to see if your drive requires defragmentation
8. If your drive need to be defragmented, then click Defragment.
9. Check your drive(s) on a regular basis.

      NOTE: Mac and Linux systems don't need to be defragmented! If you are interested in these options, see the later section on them, coming up.

Space On Your Hard Dive(s)

As we touched upon before, defragmenting your hard drive(s) is one of the most important regular maintenance tasks you should get into the habit of doing on a Windows PC. On the heels of this, and directly related is the practice of keeping ample free space on your hard drive(s) – up to 50% free is recommended.

Why? Because, as you fill up your hard drive(s), performance and speed decline. If you want your computer to run at its peek speed, always leave free space on your hard drive. It's needed for the Swap File, as well as regular system file storage.

So, keep your hard drives as bare as possible, with ample free space. You can backup to a CD/DVD, or external hard drive/flash drive to free up space on your main hard drive(s).

System Performance Settings

Window comes with animated menus and effects turned on by default. While these are pretty to look at, they do slow down you computer. We recommend to turn off any advanced effects, or menu animations.

To Turn Off Menu Effects and Animations:

1. Click on the Start Menu
2. Click Settings
3. Click on Control Panel
4. Select System
5. The System Properties window displays
6. Click the Advanced tab

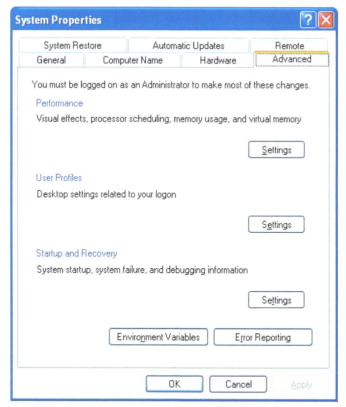

7. Click Settings in the Performance section
8. Select Adjust for best performance
9. Click OK
10. Click Apply and OK.

Windows Alternatives

There are 2 main windows alternatives these days, both of which have less need for maintenance:

- Mac (solid, stable, expensive, based on Unix)

- Linux (solid, stable, free open source software)

These operating systems **don't** tend to run more slowly after time, and their hard drives **do not** need to be defragmented on a regular basis!

This is because both the Mac and Linux systems store files differently, and run differently than a PC – that's thinking different! In fact, the Mac operating system is a variant of Unix, from which Linux shares an ancestry.

A lot of mobile devices run on Unix or a variation of Linux, because these are small and stable operating systems.

Where to find Linux versions: http://www.distrowatch.com

Regular Windows Maintenance Checklist

- Run a complete system virus and spyware scan
- Defragment your hard drive(s) when they need them
- Run C Cleaner
- Run Disk Cleanup
- Remove unneeded items from the Start Menu
- Keep the Desktop free of large files and too many icons
- Keep your browser free of unnecessary plug-ins
- Don't fill your hard dive(s) more than 50% full, if possible
- Back up your important files!

Thank you for purchasing and reading this guide from Web of Life Solutions!

We hope it will assist you in running your PC in top shape!

See our site for more of our books and services:
http://www.weboflifesolutions.com

www.ingramcontent.com/pod-product-compliance
Lightning Source LLC
Chambersburg PA
CBHW050938060326
40689CB00040B/662